THE LONG DECAY

THE LONG DECAY

AND

OTHER POEMS

BY

 BRITTA JENSON PITZL

MAPLE LAKE

2021.

For Dad—
my first reader
and most lasting impression

*"There are sleeping dreams and waking dreams;
what seems is not always as it seems."*

-Christina Georgina Rossetti

The Long Decay

I

I.

I found your letter

I found your letter
I wasn't looking for it
I didn't know about it

You wrote it before your departure
You knew you were going
You knew I would find it

I found your letter
Seven years later
You said *talk to me, I'm listening.*

This is for you.

Highway 39

Keeping schedule, I follow the dull road
onward toward commitment and routine when
my eyes halt.

A deer, wine red in the ditch
alive and glistening in the morning air
treads gently through the green.

The blazing sienna of her coat
reflects the light.
She drifts among the cattails
to someplace, to nowhere

The docile wild of her—
It lingers, like honey,
through the white noise of my mind
I feel her eyes, not in challenge,
but in sweet faith asking,

Do not the robins find shelter?
Are not the daisies fully dressed?

III.

Silver and Exact

I found my first gray hair
and I pulled it out.
Between my thumb and finger,
I twist it in the yellow bathroom light,
entranced by its translucency and strength.

Out of fear of looking my age
I tossed it— bound for the dump or
some bird's nest. I painted my nails blue.

When I turned thirty,
I found more gray hairs and I left them.
They're promise and proof that I am living—
That I didn't expire early.
The privilege of getting this far,
of knowing you this long.
A gift.

They're diamonds inlaid
on my ever expanding crown.

jamais vaisseaux partis des rives de Scamandre

ux champs Thessaliens oserent ils descendre ?

pose sur ma tête avec ses doigts

Onze lustres complets surchargés de trois ans.

BRITTA JENSON PITZL

IV.

The Long Decay

Remembering hurts
I pick at my scab
until its a scar.
It's easier to ignore, later.

I believe what I remember.
It's a long decay, like November
too deep into autumn to recall
the strawberry moon.

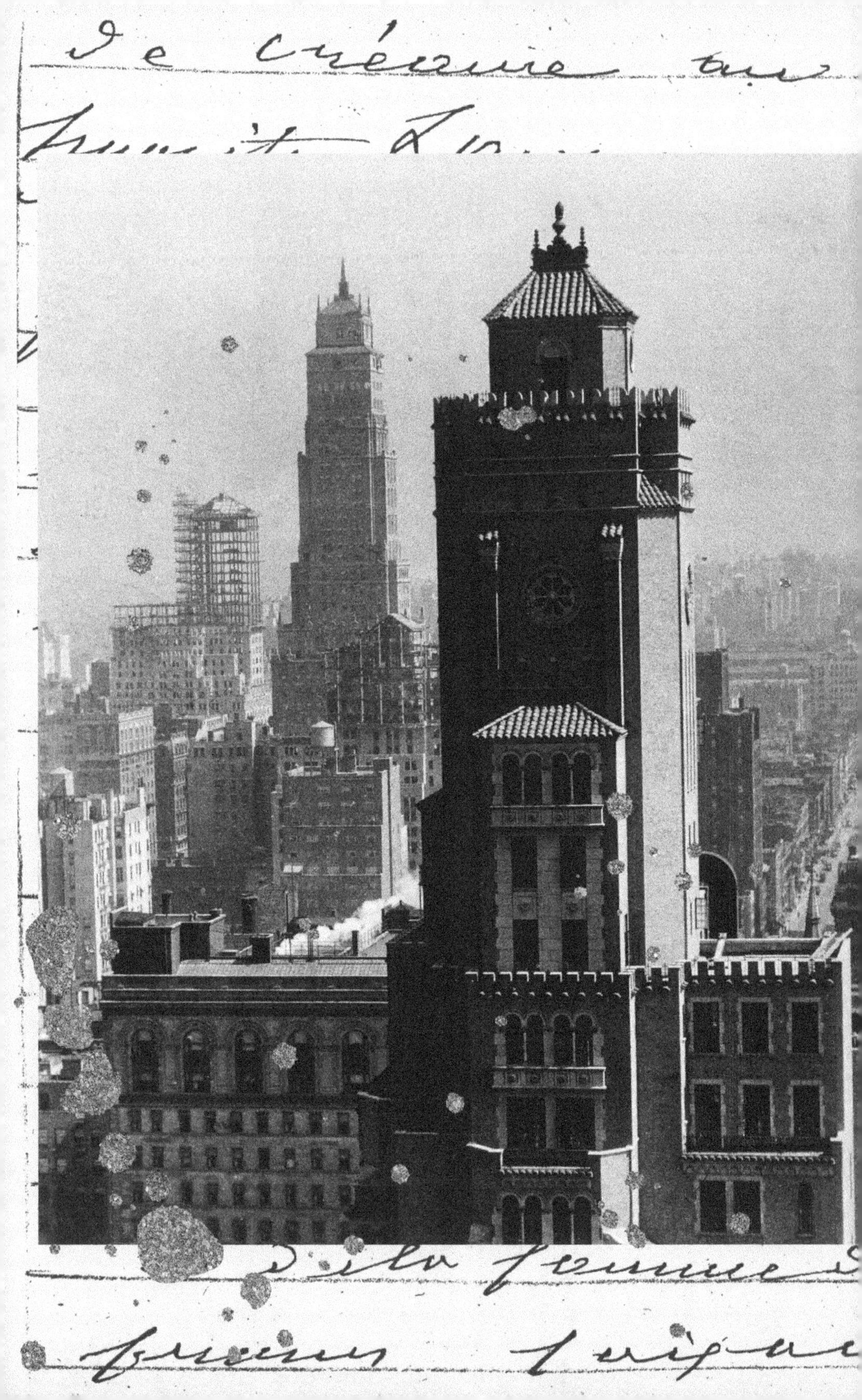

My Youth

My youth—
    far and familiar as a
hometown scent.
Hazy and intimate,
a soft breeze on my skin.

Can I return?
    Is it possible to hold a fragrance
on the tip of my tongue?
O, Unnameable Memory,
Hallowed Realm.

My youth—
    heavy and stifling
Heaving chest.
Unbearable weight,
a pound of flesh.

Can I escape?
    Will the shackles of Remembrance
grant me freedom?
O, unshakeable demon,
Midnight Dream.

Pilgrims

I wish I had lived longer
before incessant demand,
before constant availability.

I wish I had lived longer
in the age of Dillard, of Oliver, of Waldon.

When it was quiet on the frontier,
among those pioneers of the valley
crafting in silence.
Leaving a breadcrumb trail
of their lyrics,
of their Memories,
set in the amber pages in my hand.

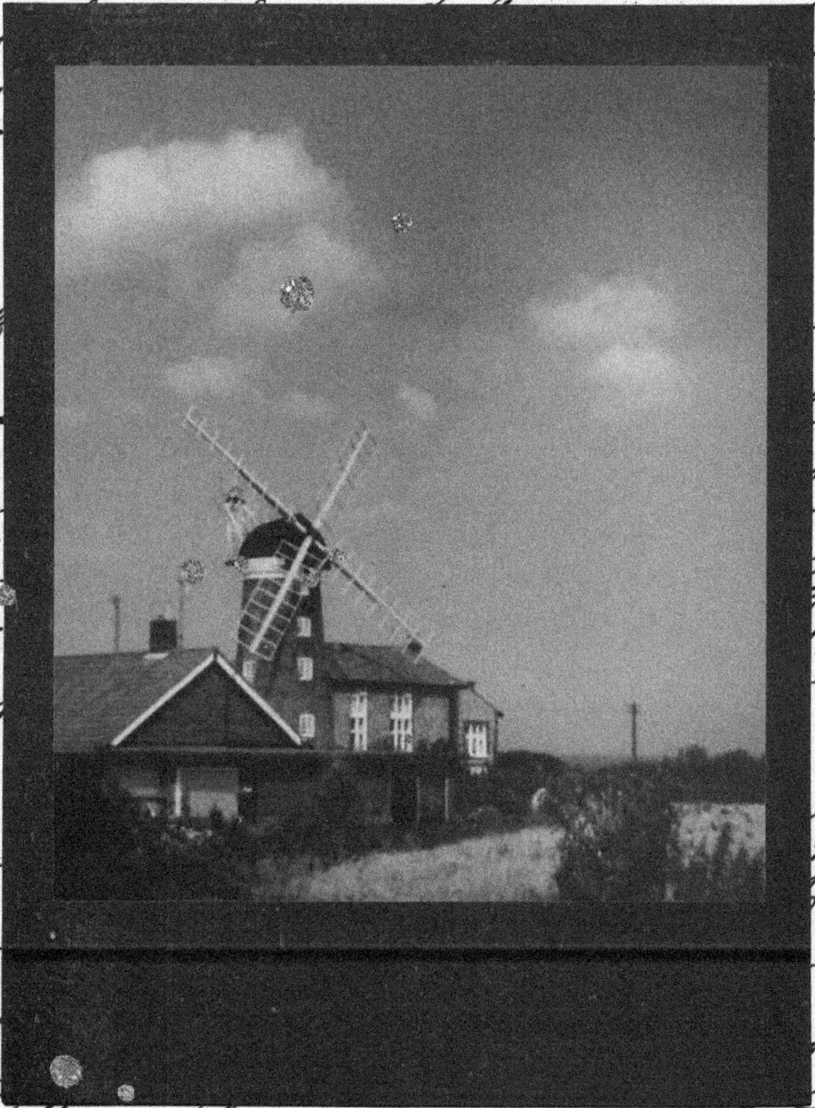

de Sernes ~~~ que de saible, qual

Mauvaises donnée le six planges que

Diners poil d'âge, d'celas aux sad venue

publet agent desd[...] vennes aux vendre

veau d'clair à suard bo vers av[...] noyer

six livres loquelle somme auroit été cinq

19 BRITTA JENSON PITZL

en pain p1o ula no riture des d'mineur

VII

30

Turning thirty looks like my bookshelf:
dreams sticky with dust and broken spines
of identities unrealized, dog-eared memories
catalogued in diaries.

Turning thirty feels like starting over:
my ink stained hand shakes from
familiar hesitation—
turning an empty raw page of a new decade,
I begin.

I am less of who I used to be
less of her, more of me.
Wondering, still, what that means.

A transition between stanzas
The pregnant pause.

VIII.

Steeped

I stop up my mouth like a tub.

It fills

    and fills

then sits. ⟲

Steeped as tea.
turning the alabaster pink,
  a stagnant stink

entirely of what I never wrote in all

    those letters.

Collecting nothing like dust,
blank paper gushing

with lack.

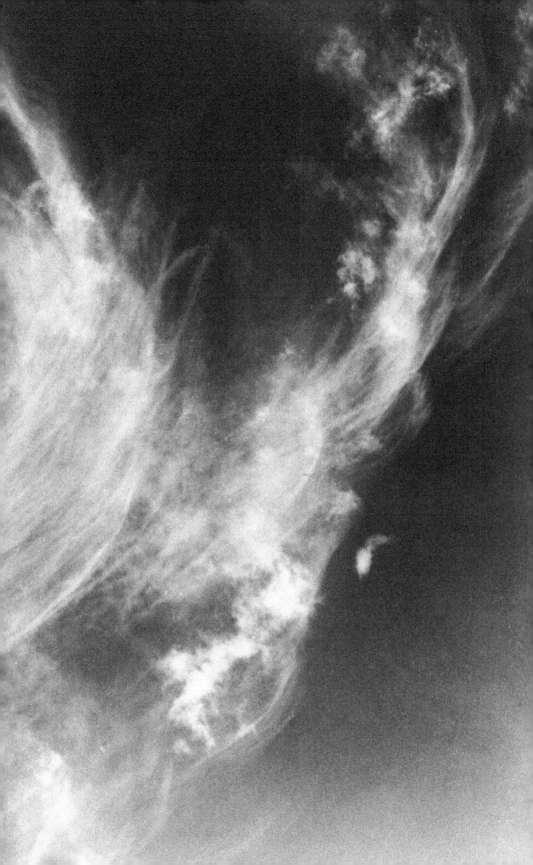

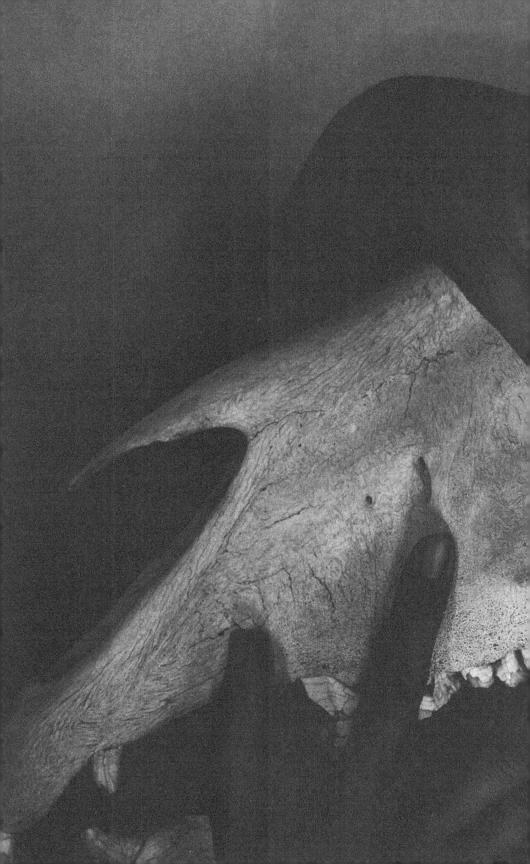

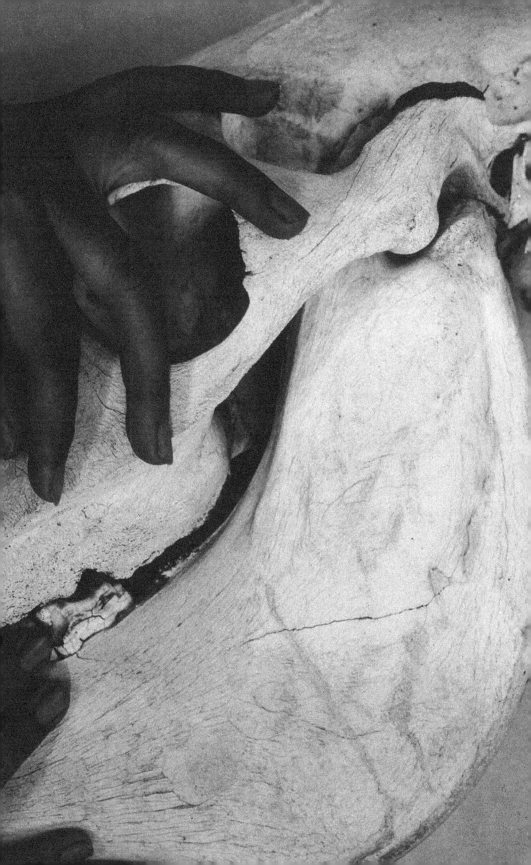

IX

Carried

I never felt so lodged
as I do in the present.
I have also never
felt so carried.

On the sidewalk ahead of of me,
I see this child, held by
the large hands and burly shoulders
of her father.

She trusts.
She knows
nothing else, no other way.
It is not a practice, to be so trusting
It is her reality— morning by morning.

Maybe I could crawl back
into my outgrown skin,
slip into soft sleeves of a sweater
and shed this weathered costume
with its scars and terror. Maybe I can
strip myself of these calloused hands,

and put on vulnerability again.

II

X.

Blizzard conditions
Mirror the cold in my heart
When will spring ever come?

XI.

Holy

The ice
breaks in sheets
layering like sweaters on a
beach of black sand beneath. I
walk on a carpet of red cedar needles,
manna from an evergreen canopy. Their
precise fingers hold up the robin egg sky,
a chorus of green and cherub clouds—
A living
cathedral
ceiling.

BRITTA JENSON PITZL

Howard Lake

This cemetery is old, the trees
are older. I feel quite at home
among these stones.

Quiet and cold under the cedar tree
the smell of October in the air,
decay in full swing.
Leaves soaked with Spring
collect on the stones
sinking into the earth with each season.

I feel as temporary as the wind.

Walking on the Moors before Evening

The graves are quiet here,
rising over tufts of green like soldiers
erect in neat rows. My pale fingers
slide across the mossed letters, cold,
clinging to the idle life of a molding stone.

Looking down grassy slopes, I am slipping
into a palpable nothing.
My shoes sink into the sponge.
My hair is in knots, I swipe at its web.

Pitch clouds are gaining ground
and the fear is setting in. Here comes the rain
clawing at my chest, my hands, my eyes.

Absorbed into the soft grass,
my secrets sink deeper
into the earth.

8

Permanent

The night is a murmur
holding in the quiet, like armor.
White, thick as honey
laughs from the sky in bursts

Pulling the faux fur on the hood
of my coat closer
to my brittle cheeks I feel
the bite of winter's dust.

I take smaller steps thinking
it'll get me there faster.
I breathe in all the lesser,
avoiding December's sting.

I am none the warmer.

Almost—

It was almost ours:
Brass doorknobs worn by centuries,
the face of the city
scarred by history.

It was almost ours:
River walks, arm in arm
long nights and a bottle of wine
under the willow tree.

The absolute impermanence of fantasy
prevented even us from fucking up.

It just wasn't ours to keep.

The nature of oceans is to separate
The nature of stars is to cross.

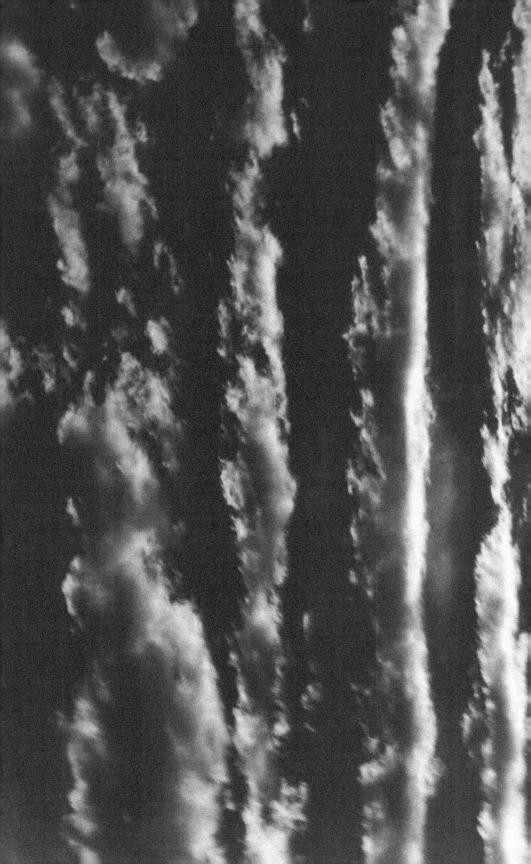

XVI.

Don't Wake Me

Perpetual, as slow steady rain,
  I erode, so easily
  it looks like living.

Alcohol and Ambien numb away pain,
  heavy sleeper,
  evading morning.

Tomorrow comes early,
  same absurd tune.
  I pull the covers over my head.

I replay my dreams like a song
  because tomorrow won't begin
  if the night stays long.

XVII

When It's Over

If you're going to let me go,
let me go gentle, but plain.
Don't make me a fool.

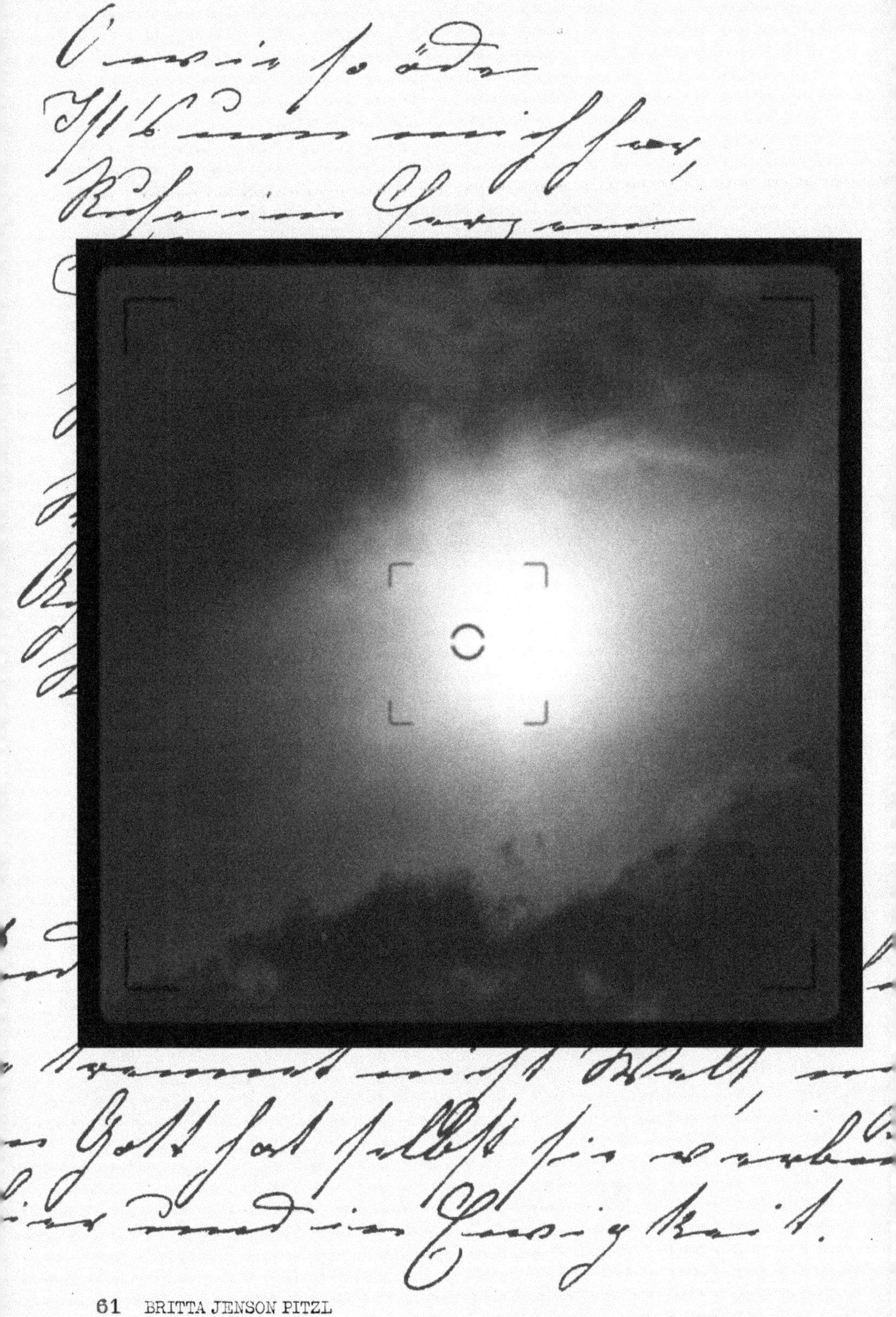

Hard Times

The winter winds drove us inside; midnight at Hard Times
Crowded with sticky tables and good company
What kept us there— a perpetual fault line
in the stars, under a cold moon, tragically unaligned.

A Drunk Poet

A drunk poet is a dangerous one
  because she'll reveal her tricks
  in whispers

All the words you've said to her,
  now memorized, immortalized,
  lyrics that swim in her veins—
  living poetry.

Nothing's sweeter than
  the sound of your own
  n-a-m-e.

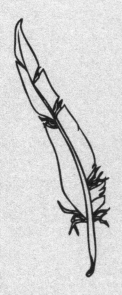

Ancien Noël

XX.

Bruised—

We drink in a pulsating cauldron.
This sloshing Burgundy in hand, we are
elbowed into the hallway

By opening a window, will it bleed out?
Can I escape through the rush of red?
And land among the loitering and anonymous
conversations lit by the rose
of their cigarettes?

XXI

Civil Wars

Diesel hung in the wet London air
where I found her house
just south of the zoo.

Were her hands shaking as she
stuffed towels under doors of her children's rooms,
or did she have the calm of a cat,
belly full, preparing for a long snooze?

On the stoop outside, I examine
my dirty fingernails and
I imagine her Poet hands ⟶
turning on the gas.

BRITTA JENSON PITZL

XXII.

Evening

I'll be quite comfortable
leaving my body here
in cool, green sheets
and with the robin's
lullabies between their beaks.

I seek solitude only
graveyards keep.

III

XXIII.

Empty skies of spring
Birds know now it is their time
Winter's clutch is strong

tres et Escritures restés dans le domicille dudit feu

…bled apres son decés ainsy quén tous autres lieux

…las veuve tutrice auroit connoissance quil

…une cremaillere, un gril, une grille un

trepied Le tout de fer, Item deux Marmittes de

potin avec une Escueille a tremper La soupe -

une poesle d'erain denviron quatre livre,

XXIV.

My Father Lay Dying

I was in Yankton, where summer came early and with
school out, I felt carefree for the first time in a
while. Back home, my dad was dying from brain
cancer in a hospice care center in St. Paul. I figured
one weekend away wouldn't hurt. The sun turned the grass
yellow and my friends and I drove down to the beach where
the sloshing of the Missouri River was enough to make
your mouth water. I made sure to Instagram enough of my
trip to show everyone back home that I was having fun. I
shoved my phone in the pocket of my black short-shorts
and followed my friends to the edge of the sand where the
bridge to Nebraska stretched south.

Maneuvering our awkward bodies to the ledge of the
bridge foundation, we sat, legs hanging, side by side.
This was unusual behavior for me, to be so adventur-
ous. When I stood up, however, my phone leapt from my
too-small-women's-short-short pocket and flew graceful-
ly, like an Olympic swimmer off a diving board, into the
river. Plop. Gone. Everything. Every picture, every text,
every contact. Any chance of my mom calling me and tell-
ing me if my dad was still alive, gone. Except that her
phone number is the only one I had memorized so I used
my friend's phone to let her know my current unfortunate
circumstance. The rest of the day was a blur.

That night I found myself with strangers among my
friends, several 12 packs of beer, and a makeshift fire
on the clay shore of the river, under a pine crowned
cliff. I sipped a Pabst as this guy tried to convince
me to come over and drink moonshine with him. I told him
my dad was dying as we speak and I wasn't interested. I
clicked open another beer.

Eventually the cops found us because it's illegal to
make fires on this piece of state property. Everyone under 21 got a breathalyzer test. Once I got to the place I
was staying, the realization that I was drunk, away from
home, and left my mother with my dying father, hit me.
I sobbed on the basement bathroom tile floor, my friend
holding me.

The next morning I woke with puffy eyes and combed
my hair for church. In the church lobby, I held a donut
in one hand and burnt coffee in another, making small
talk with some old ladies. One of my friends walked
up to me, saying my mom texted, asking me to call. My
stomach dropped. I said no. If I waited until after the
service, then it wasn't real yet. It wouldn't be real
until I called back. Life was the same until I called.
I was still a daughter of a father until I called. In
the sanctuary, the congregation sang "I'll fly away,
O glory, I'll fly away." I wept until we had to shake
hands with the person in the row behind us. Back at the
house, I called my mom. She said that at 9:30 a.m. he
flew away, O glory.

Later, my friends and I had lunch with the pastor
at a Mexican Restaurant. He was a jolly man who talk-
ed a lot. The enchilada on my plate sat untouched and
I pushed rice from one side of the plate to the other.
The long table was filled with the pastor's family, my
friend's relations. The old man asked me about my
mom's line of work and I told him. He asked me about my
dad's line of work. I told him. Mistakenly, I used past
tense words when describing my dad. Words like "had"
and "worked." He caught on to my grammatical choices.
He pressed, "You used the past tense. Is your father no
longer part of your life?" I should have lied. I said
he died. He said "Oh, I'm so sorry. When?" I said "This
morning." He stared at me.

My chair scratched against the red tile floor as I
ran to the bathroom, ashamed of my own compulsive need
to choose accuracy over tact. I realized it was the
first time I had said it aloud. It was real.
I retched.

XXV.

Oct.

this time of year I am gentle,
succumbed to an old grief
a continuous June gloom.
I see my breath this afternoon on the cold humid air,
the weight of it held after rain.

Its funny how we romanticize death.
Instagram the autumn leaves because they're beautiful.
How grateful you are that this world has Octobers.)

Its funny how we romanticize death.
Feel the leaves beneath your feet.
Tweet about the pumpkin flavor between your teeth.)

Once he left, I've lived in a perpetual October
and I've discovered
that grief is
walking into the wind.

It's a scent
I've grown accustomed to.
I no longer romanticize death.
Now, it's my everyday perfume.

XXVI

6/22/14

John Mayer played through the aux cord
on the long drive home. I lay in the back of
the car, staring at the sky through the sunroof
and sang badly and unashamed because a
part of me died that day too.
    We pulled over just over the border to stretch
our legs and found a partially
submerged bench on the flooded beach. He grabbed
his guitar, she grabbed a couple
cigarettes, and the three of us sat, hip to hip,
our feet dangling over the water and he
smoked while strumming "Slow Dancing"
as the sun made her bed.
    Later, I pulled into the parking lot
of my suburban apartment complex at midnight,
and texted the boy I loved, "he died today."
    He called me, but I drank myself to sleep.

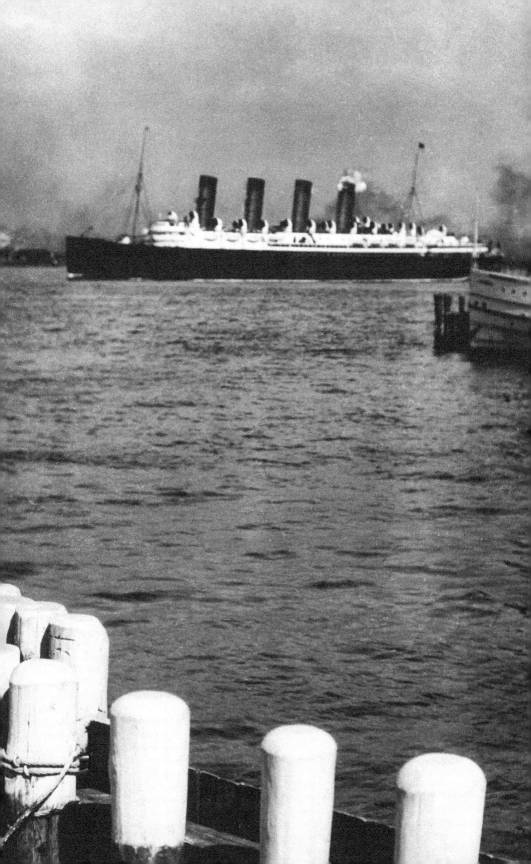

XXVII

Garden

I planted a garden so I had a future
to believe in.
Pulling intrusive thoughts like weeds
I (tried) to stay sane.

But the city is burning
and it feels like its all ending
again. You slip your hand into mine.
Though I've succumbed to hopelessness,
you're still by my side.
You don't promise me a bouquet,
but you promise that you'll stay.

You can't kiss the sadness away but
Try, oh god, try.

XXVIII.

Stillborn

I wasn't there to catch you
when you fell out of bed.
The sticky ooze of your cocoon
collects seeds and dirt,
decorating your wound with jewels.

In my hand I saw the glue that holds you,
the translucent yolk yields no warmth for your
forming bones. Your mother grieves, openly,
from the woods, a world too violent for your purity.

XXIX

Liturgy

I picked up a book of poetry,
a cup of tea and
I read it, three times.
Imaginary rosary,
fumbling over each word hoarsely,
praying their beauty over me.

I read this one slowly,
so it'll always feel new.
I read this one slowly,
so I'll be astounded afresh.

I step outside and open my eyes wider.
I turn my face towards the East.

Devotion.

Night Retreats

Night retreats
so I untangle my legs from the sheets,
brew my tea and wrap
myself in the past,
warm as my cardigan.

Staring at soft curves of cream,
I'm remembering this
porcelain dream—

Thirty years gone,
the gritty page, like lemonade,
weathered with age, browning with time,
in your hands. My poetry in your mouth and
your handwriting in my margins.

I stroke the memory slowly,
trying to stay in that sweet

in between state
  of dreams and
    being awake.

Hiraeth

Standing in your doorway, I hesitate.
I examine the white paint, cracked eggshell that
flakes under my finger tips,
chipped as my nail polish, falling gently
to the carpet.

Daring to touch the worn door handle
glossy from many year's grip,
I can't convince myself to turn it.

Dumbly, I stand there,
remembering the palpable silence
of that November night,
sobbing goodbye into your shoulder
breathing in the fibers of your sweater.

Instead, I shove the letter under the door,
pull up my scarf, and brave the December air.

BRITTA JENSON PITZL

XXXII.

Overdue

In your sweater, bruise blue,
stiff collar peeking through,
you stood there,
asking me which cufflinks you should choose
"That one," I pointed,
pretending I knew.

Sunday morning, I take the cup,
mouthing prayers on cue.
I savor these moments
because this ending is overdue,
and you knew.

You knew.

XXXIII

Ricochet

I hope you saw my mascara running.
I wore it just for you.

The jet black stream carrying south my dignity,
smeared on your shoulder.

This affliction,
I feel its talons in the undertow,
sense its malignity

I dissolved into you like salt in water.
You held me up like the Dead Sea.

Sunlight dances in the passenger seat
  and I'm missing you.

I love you, I loved you.
Oh, how I ricochet.

IV

XXXIV

Warm as August's breeze
Breath on my neck gives me chills
I fear summer's end

XXXV.

Morning Breath

She's turning her thoughts.
An endless pacific against rock—
white noise that won't stop.
An eastern crack of blue
sears through sticky air
and untamed hair

She awoke from her wintering,
all hope and fantasy
on the tip of her tongue and the rim of her
coffee.

Item une quittance Expediée par Ledit deffunt à
Madelaine Surbled sa belle mere Contenant
plusieurs dispositionde devant nous Susdit

novembre mil sept cens trente cinq cotté 19
Item cinq quittances Expediées par diverses

particulierde audit deffunt de differents jours

Item une Remise de ladite piece faite par
ledit Jean Surbled audit deffunt passé devant nous
…udit Gouel Le vingt-six de mars mil septcent…

…urier mil septcent trente huit — cotte 8 et 9.
Item une quittance expédiée par Jean Surbled audit deffunt …
…de la somme de trente deux livres en datte du dix huit mars mil septcent…
…arante cotté 10.

TIMBRE IMPERIAL
cen. 50.
Inscription d'hypothèque judiciaire
marchand boulanger demeurant
La présente prise en renouvellement de celle inscrite au
bureau le vingt un décembre mil huit cent cinquante cinq

XXXVI.

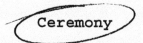

Ceremony

On the edge of the sea, under the oak tree
you're standing under a teal sky,
raising a hand to your mouth
inhaling in a slow drag.

Scalloped lace curls around my ankles,
brushing against the generous earth
I meet you at the surf, where the grass kisses
the beach and for a brief moment, our mouths meet.

Through white plumes from your lips
you quote Sylvia, exceptionally well.
Where once there was death, now plays love.

XXXVII.

Sacred Hours

Breakfast with you feels like home.
Sticky mouths sipping coffee,
I steal glances over the rim, reading you.
Folding the paper, I get up to refill my cup
and you motion me closer.

We kiss.

And then the wind blows and
you're off to work and
the day fades into blue and
I want to
recreate those sacred early hours
with you

over and
over and
over.

XXXVIII.

Sapling

My love, sometimes I imagine two of you—
your clumsy shadow.
Another pair of skinny legs and head full
of your same wispy white hair,
bleached by the sun.

Bright sea foam eyes, busy bee,
a mouth always singing.
With dirty knees on the forest floor,
looking upwards.

Our little sapling.

XXXIX.

August

Autumn's first light
comes in the morning
Breath off the lake.

White pines, weathered and weary
weave around red roads
Their wide brimmed hats, hazy and blue.

A superior awakening—
The yolk of the moon lingers this morning
summer rubs the sleep from her eyes

Like a lover who reaches over
to touch your face, holding
on to the *not just yet*—

the in between.

58

XL.

Conversation with the Pacific

"I have you," say the waves, with
each lick of the shore.

"Don't you see me?" I scream.

"I have you," say the waves, with
each lick of the shore.

"You are incomprehensible. Don't you see me?"
I scream.

"I have you," says the waves, with
each lick of the shore.

"You have me," I say, collapsing under the current
of being known.

Savor the silence of fog.
Believe beyond what's seen— even if you have to crawl.

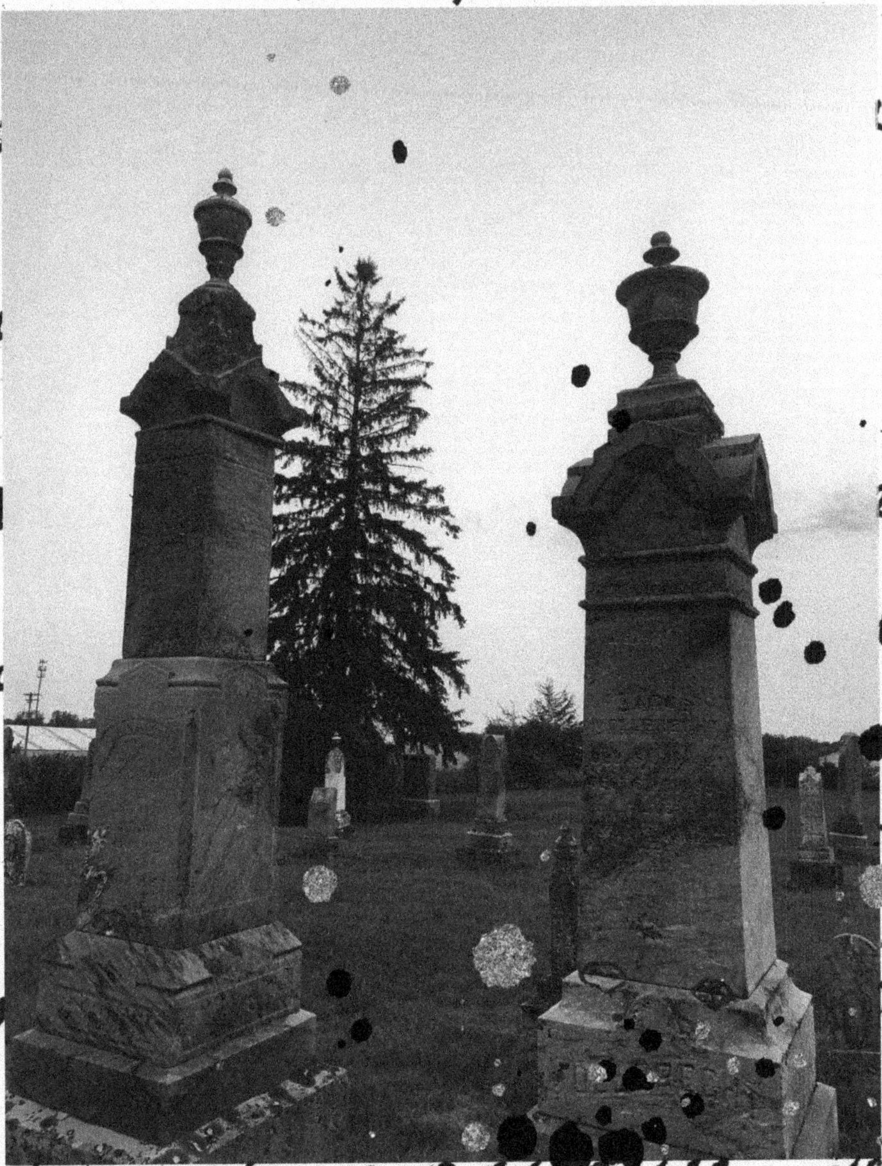

table ou établie à

billot un autre

un œil fort depuis d'être

Index

I found your letter   1
Highway 39   4
Silver and Exact   5
The Long Decay   8
My Youth   14
Pilgrims   15
30   20
Steeped   21
Carried   29
Holy   36
Walking on the Moors before Evening   41
Permanent   50
Almost—   51
Don't Wake Me   56
When It's Over   57
Hard Times   62
A Drunk Poet   63
Bruised—   68
Civil Wars   69
Evening   74
My Father Lay Dying   79
Oct.   84
6/22/14   85
Garden   92
Stillborn   98
Liturgy   99
Night Retreats   104
Hiraeth   105
Overdue   108
Ricochet   113
Morning Breath   122
Ceremony   126
Sacred Hours   127
Sapling   134
August   135
Conversation with the Pacific   142
     Acknowledgments   162
     About the Poet   164

Ich hab dich lieb …

Dich … tausend … Mal!

Durch Wald … Dorf, durch … und Dorn …

… Jäger …

Da … Nacht … …

Die Mägde … …

Der Jäger … …

… er … …

Der Fischer … Netz ins Meer

Und fing … zum … Ruderschlage;

Ich … …

Die … … …

Ich hab … … grüße

Dich … tausend Mal!

Spielmanns Lied

Und legt ihr zwischen mich und sie
Auch Wasser und Thal und Hügel,
Gestrenge Herren, ihr trennt uns nie,
Das Lied, das Lied hat Flügel.

Ich bin ein [...] Notes [...] allbekannt,
Ich mach mich auf die Reise
Und sing heut fort durch manche Land
[...] nach die einen Weise.

Ich hab dich lieb, die Süße
die meine Lust und Qual,
Ich hab dich lieb und grüße
dich tausend, tausend Mal.

Der kleine Bach belebt auch Noch der Müh'!
Sei Gut! Sei Gut!

Was Moses, Christus, Sokrates gelehrt,
Was alle andern Weisheit auch erklärt.
Ich hab als Kernpunkt Eines nur gefunden
Und an die Wahrheit treu mein Herz gebunden
Woraus des Menschen ... allein besteht.
Sei Gut ...

Und fragt Ihr ... ... letzter Trost,
der Lohn, auf die ... ... Er?
Was soll ich sorgen ... ... Welten
Und einst ... ... vergelten?
Mir lebt ... ... Blick!
Sei ... ...

Des fremden ... ... Christ.

Es läuft ein fremdes Kind
Am Abend vor Weihnachten
Durch die Stadt geschwind,
die Lichter zu betrachten,
die angezündet sind.

Date:

Doch wie sich die Paare schwangen
In der Abendsonnengold
Rind auf meine dunklen Wangen
Heiße Thränen herabgerollt.

Ach, ich dachte bei dem Sange
An des Vaters ...
Wie in trübem Mondesglanze
Freier abend ...
Wo sich bei der ...
Jeder Fuß behende ...
Und der Knabe in ...
Glühend den Fandango schlingt.

Nein! das ... schwerd schlagen
Länger hält ... nicht zurück.
Will ja jeder Lust entsagen,
Laßt mir nur ... ... Glück
Fort zum Süden ...
In das Land wo ... !
Unterm ... ...
Muß ich ... begraben ...

Emanuel Geibel.

Date:

Allerseelen.

Date:

Bleibt dir ein Freundesherz, so bist du reich,
Und wär' der höchsten ... ... geworden
Und keinen Freund hat ... ...

F. M. ...

Gedenksprüchlein.

Sei Gut! so sagt oft ... ...,
der ... ... der Erde Grund,
Sei Gut! so klingt ... ... die Ohren,
— Das kleine ... ... verloren, —
Als ... ...

Sei ...

... ...,
... ...,
... ... Recht zu halten,
Nach eigner Willkür, ... Lust zu schalten,
Der kleine ... bleibt ... ... der ...

Sei Gut! Sei Gut!

Und ... der ... ... dem Herzen geht
Das ... will das ganze Leben ...,
Daß, ach! so ... Menschen unerfüllet!
... ... bleibt mir ...

Date:

Ein jeder Vater denkt,
Den ... auf seine Kinder,
Die Mutter ... beschenkt,
Denkt ... ...
An ... — ... Niemand ...

O lieber ... ...
Nicht ... ... Vater
Hab' ich ... ... bist,
O, sei ... ...
... ... vergißt

Das ... ... die Hand,
... ist vor Freude erstarret,
Es ... ...
Und ... der ... harret,
Der Blick hinaufgewandt.

Date:

Acknowledgments

Thank you Travis, my husband. You are my motivator and constant companion. Thank you for listening to me read, complain, celebrate, and laugh. I love you.

Thank you Laura Harris for being my cheerleader and the first to hold my manuscript. Pouring over every poem at the coffeeshop and staying there past closing time on the patio discussing God, poetry, and the universe will always be one of my favorite memories with you. You're the loveliest person I know.

Thank you Nick Wiese for your time, energy, and wisdom in helping me edit these poems. I cannot express enough thanks. I respect you so much.

Thank you to Greta Valentine for hosting weekly writing sessions which kept me on track. Your encouragement and friendship means the world to me.

About the Poet

   Britta Jenson Pitzl graduated from North Central University with a bachelors degree in English Literature and has been writing poetry since she was ten years old. She lives with her husband, Travis in the heart of Minnesota. This is her debut book.

Follow her journey on Instagram:
@brittajensonpitzl

ILLUSTRATION & PHOTO CREDITS: Thank you to
the New York Public Library, Library of
Congress, Biodiversity Heritage Library,
and many more libraries around the world
for keeping gorgeous centuries-old photog-
raphy and illustrations accessible & avail-
able for viewing and use through Public
Domain. Special thanks to rawpixel for dig-
itally enhancing many vintage images.
Featured Photographer: Alfred Stieglitz
(1864-1946)
All images sourced
through CC0 license.

Printed in the USA
CPSIA information can be obtained
at www.ICGtesting.com
JSHW040748030823
45812JS00006B/230